Tiny

essentials of
an effective
volunteer board

Other books by the author

Advertising by Charities, Directory of Social Change, London 1984.

Charity Annual Reports, Directory of Social Change, London 1986.

Relationship Fundraising, The White Lion Press, London 1992.

Friends for Life: Relationship Fundraising in Practice, The White Lion Press, London 1996.

How to Produce Inspiring Annual Reports, Directory of Social Change, London 2000 (with Karin Weatherup and the Burnett Works Company).

Relationship Fundraising revised and expanded second edition, Jossey-Bass Inc, San Francisco 2002.

The Zen of Fundraising, Jossey-Bass Inc, San Francisco (to be published in March 2006).

Tiny

White Lion
Press

essentials of
an effective
volunteer board

by Ken Burnett

Published by
The White Lion Press Limited
567 Ben Jonson House
The Barbican
London
EC2Y 8NH

© 2006 Ken Burnett/The White Lion Press Limited
ISBN 0-9518971-8-7

First printed 2006

British Library Cataloguing-in-Publication Data.
A catalogue record for this book is available from the
British Library.

Models: Paul Hessey, Roger Lawson and Jaz Nannar

Photography by Adrian Taylor

Design and print production by *e*m associates

Printed and bound by CPI Group (UK) Ltd,
Croydon, CR0 4YY

Contents

The author

In addition to nearly three decades' experience as a fundraiser, consultant, director and chairman of a number of companies, Ken Burnett has served on several volunteer boards, including the executive committee of the UK Institute of Fundraising, the board of the International Fund Raising Group (now The Resource Alliance), the council of BookAid International and the board of trustees of ActionAid International, one of the world's most progressive and most influential international non-government organisations. He was vice-chair of the Institute of Fundraising for two years and from 1998 to 2003 he was chairman of trustees of ActionAid. In January 2006 he was invited back onto the board of ActionAid International after a break of one year.

If you would like to find out more about Ken Burnett please visit

www.kenburnett.com and www.whitelionpress.com

Preface

Hardly any volunteer boards are perfect. Some, we know, work really well and quite a few are truly excellent. But they remain the exceptions. Many boards function reasonably enough (assuming you believe that merely 'good enough' is anywhere near good enough for your organisation). In our experience most, if not all of the rest add little value to their organisation and are as likely to be a barrier to progress as a force for change, a liability for their cause as much as an asset.

The short cast of characters who appear in this little tale are deliberate caricatures, not intended to resemble any individual living or dead. Instead they are composites of many. Readers will surely identify one or more people from their personal acquaintance who rejoice in similar characteristics or attributes to Camilla, or Arthur, or Ron. Or David, Serena, or Theresa.

For most voluntary organisations identifying, recruiting and developing a truly effective board remains a wonderful but usually distant and elusive dream. This small book has been written for all board members and nonprofit staff whose job it is to deal with 'the board'. Its purpose is to help any board do its important job better.

Praise for *Tiny Essentials of an Effective Volunteer Board*

'Entertaining and paced like a thriller novel… how to avoid the perils and pitfalls of nonprofit governance to find the undoubted treasure that is an effective volunteer board.'
Salil Shetty, director, United Nations Millennium Development Goals Campaign, New York, USA.

'This book is completely relevant for American nonprofits, and the British tone is what, for me, made it so readable. It is like a grand mystery in the Agatha Christie tradition… I loved the language as much as the content. It's a hit!'
Jennie Thompson, former chair, The Resource Alliance and consultant, Washington DC, USA.

'Lots of wry truths and sharp observations wrapped up in a tiny package – so much will ring true and loudly to chairs and CEOs of non-profit organisations worldwide. The wisdom is conveyed with such cogency and understanding, this tiny book is sure to become a transformational must-read for new chairs and well-established boards alike. I'm going to circulate it to my chair and trustees.'
James Partridge OBE, founder and chief executive, Changing Faces, London, UK.

'How refreshing! An insightful, practical guide to good governance; its content far outweighs its size. There are very many nuggets of good practice, immersed in experiences we can relate to. Frightening, frustrating and fumbling figures from my past re-emerge in the pages of this tiny book, alongside the honourable, sensible practices that contribute so much to making not-for-profit organisations all they aspire to become.'
Dr John R Batten MBE, founder and director general, the Poverty Eradication Network, Nairobi, Kenya.

Author's note

Some North American friends whose opinions I respect have said that this little book is far too British and that many American readers won't understand the British terminology, phrases and sayings. Other friends from across the Atlantic whose opinions I respect just as much, told me not to change a word; its Britishness is its charm.

What's an author to do?

The action in this brief account unquestionably takes place in Britain. While the lessons they convey are universal, the caricatures are undoubtedly very British. I felt on reflection that removing or diluting the British-isms might risk blandness, so I've decided to keep them in. While to some the words in a few places may seem strange, the meaning is mostly self-evident from the context. And if it's not, please go to the publisher's website www.whitelionpress.com for a glossary of idiosyncratic British terms. I'm sure that readers will find any elusive meaning there – and probably lots more besides.

Also, I use the term 'volunteer board' to describe the governing bodies of charities, nonprofits and similar organisations.

A new chair

Warren Maxwell's life is about to change – dramatically. He's soon to be propelled from a life of comfort and complacency into a journey of discovery, change and transformation. He will find it interesting and informative, but it won't be comfortable or easy. It will, however, give him a great deal of satisfaction.

Warren is 43 years old and a former social worker who now runs his own consultancy business. He's a friendly, energetic, outgoing individual who enjoys life; he works and plays reasonably hard and is a conscientious member of his community. By any definition Warren is a busy man, but not so busy, he hopes, that he can't find time to take a lively interest in the world or do something to help others.

While pouring most of his energy into building up his small but growing firm Warren tries to maintain a sensible balance between his work and family life. He's been married to Joyce for 14 years and they have two sons Darren, 12 and Simon, nine. Warren keeps fit, enjoys a few hours two or three times each week in his local hostelry and doesn't go to church as often as he, or to be more accurate, Joyce, thinks he should. A liberal free-thinker with political leanings towards the left, Warren is really quite conservative in his lifestyle and average in most things. If pressed he would claim unselfconsciously that he is happy and fulfilled. That, he would confidently assert, is 'the main thing'. His now not-so-new business, once a source of some anxiety, is showing signs that it will soon mature into a reasonably lucrative and not too demanding enterprise, which suits Warren nicely because he feels that there has to be more to life than work. So now he's also able to return to another love of his life, teaching social work part-time at the local university.

But as chance would have it, in addition to all this there's another work interest in Warren's life these days, one that's about to become a whole lot more challenging, demanding and interesting.

For some time now Warren has served as a trustee on the board of FuturePoint, a national charity working to rehabilitate young offenders. This voluntary role came about by accident, through an introduction from the father of a friend of his son Darren, who'd got into trouble with the law (the friend, not his father). Darren's friend's dad had been on the board of FuturePoint for a few years and he persuaded Warren that his social work experience equipped him ideally for this 'honestly not very demanding' role.

Although it indeed turned out not to be onerous, Warren nevertheless sees this volunteer role as his 'bit', something he does from duty without complaining. He does it because somewhere in his subconscious he feels it's the kind of thing a well-rounded, middle-class adult like him should do.

It's his opportunity to help others less fortunate than him and his.

FuturePoint is a medium-sized, fairly high profile organisation doing good work with some really difficult cases. The charity can demonstrate impressive results and has many success stories to tell. Warren's happy to be involved with them. Meagre though it may be in terms of the time and effort he contributes, it's his opportunity to 'put something back' to help others less fortunate than him and his. He feels good about being on FuturePoint's board, although his attendance at meetings is merely average and he usually keeps his head down so as not to reveal that he hasn't properly read the board papers. Warren likes being a trustee and enjoys his role, which, with meetings just four times a year, always in London, doesn't put many additional demands on his already busy lifestyle. His position as a trustee reflects well on him in his other, paid, part-time role, as visiting lecturer in social work at the university. And it gives him and his students useful course material.

Now, after three interesting but undemanding years as a backbench trustee of FuturePoint, Warren has had a considerable shock. His chairman has unexpectedly resigned and, much to his surprise and consternation, Warren finds himself nominated for the vacant post of chair and put under some pressure by an informal subgroup of his fellow trustees to accept. He suspects each of the other trustees is anxious to avoid the task, so they have conspired together to find a safe pair of hands into which the charity's fate can be placed for the present. His appointment, he's sure, will be secure only for as long as it will take for a properly constituted subcommittee of the board to find a prominent figurehead suitable to be chair long term.

Warren knows there are good boards and bad boards and that while his isn't dysfunctional, as yet, it probably veers more towards ineffective than highly effective. Indeed he's often wondered to himself why the board exists, what value it adds and how the organisation would function without it. On this last point, he suspects, FuturePoint might well do rather better than it is at present. It might even prosper and become truly effective.

After some heart-searching Warren decides to accept the offered crown, but not as a sinecure. He thinks it's high time his charity got the high quality board it deserves. He can see that an invigorated board might lead to dramatic and welcome changes in the organisation as a whole. And he accepts, somewhat unwillingly, that he just might be the right person to lead this major change. But first, he realises, he needs to learn a lot more – and quickly – about what makes a truly effective volunteer board, beyond what common sense dictates and the little he knows already from experience.

Three visits

Warren's predecessor as chair having left rather suddenly, Warren finds himself in the hot seat from the moment he agrees to take over. By coincidence his appointment has come just four weeks after the chief executive has left for a senior government role, so one of Warren's first priorities is to play a part in finding a successor for the CEO. Although this means both chair and CEO will be new to their jobs at the same time, several of the other trustees have assured Warren this is all to the good.

'This way you can be sure we recruit someone you can work with', said one of them. 'Better you make your own mistakes than have to inherit someone else's.'

This didn't sound too comforting to Warren. The CEO is the only staff member to attend board meetings and, together with the chair, he (or now, thought Warren radically, perhaps even 'she') is expected to do most of the work that is necessary to give the board at least the semblance of functionality. He reflected on the turbulent, disaffected senior management team the new CEO will inherit and on several other challenges he knows will be coming his or her way. Surely such a novice team will be at a considerable disadvantage?

With no handover period from his predecessor and no induction period plus, despite loud protestations to the contrary, almost no tangible support from his fellow trustees, Warren decides to visit a few other nonprofit boards to see what he can learn from what they do. He hopes that through this he'll unearth some guidelines of 'best practice', although, from what he's heard over the past three years about how other nonprofit boards function, he isn't too optimistic about learning much that he doesn't know already.

Nevertheless, grasping his courage and his briefcase in both hands, Warren decides initially to visit just three other voluntary organisations with similar-sized boards to his, to see what he can learn.

A weak board

The man with the greasy hair and crumpled suit opposite Warren seemed far more confident than his appearance suggested he deserved to be.

'Our chairman, Lord Weatherspoon, sends his apologies', he announced, 'he's indisposed. But I can tell you all that you need to know about our board.'

This was Arthur, the chief executive officer of the Overseas Support Agency. Arthur went on to explain that he's been chief executive for the past 25 years and seemed rather keen to dispel any illusions Warren might be suffering from, that in Lord W's absence he'd been palmed off with a mere subordinate and a commoner to boot. In fact, Arthur seemed determined to compensate for his lack of title and apparently more junior status by assuring Warren that he, Arthur, is really the power at the OSA and that his chairman almost invariably fails to turn up when he says he will and even when he does he, Arthur, pulls all the strings.

Arthur went on to explain that he has presided over considerable growth in his organisation and is no stranger to success or accomplishment. But recently things have got tough, there are just too many other charities around doing the same work and during the last 10 years his organisation has declined steadily.

'But we're still doing all right', Arthur claimed, 'all things considered. Still doing a good job, even though some downsizing is inevitable. These are hard times for most organisations in overseas development, particularly as the government is doing so little and there are more poor people now than ever before. It's a wonder we've survived.'

The board, he went on to say, is 'really OK, not a problem at all'. Some very big names, he claimed, sat on the OSA board – and he reeled off a few titles from the ranks of the 'great and the good', some of whom Warren recognised as also on the boards of several other national charities. However Arthur quickly pointed out that, '… you can't expect people like that to turn up often for the likes of our meetings, though, can you?'

'Frankly', he continued, 'most of our trustees are sweethearts, real treasures. They don't interfere because it only shows off their ignorance. I manage them very carefully of course. Like recently – this'll make you laugh, I can tell you.'

At this point Arthur leaned conspiratorially towards Warren, 'In one of our recent meetings, after the usual stuff like the minutes and matters arising and the other bits and bobs, you know, any other business and what have you, we had just two substantive items on the agenda, the opening of our new development programme in Burundi, Central Africa and the relocation of our charity thrift shop in Grimsby, Yorkshire.

'Well – listen to this – we spent less than two minutes discussing Burundi, because none of the board had any idea of where it is or what goes on there so the new programme was approved "on the nod", even though it's costing us thousands. But they'd all been to Grimsby and they all had opinions on which side of the High Street is best for a charity shop. So we debated that back and forth, back and forth for about 20 minutes before I got my way in the end.'

Arthur paused for breath and took a long swig from the mug of tea they'd each been given at the start of their meeting. 'But they're not a bad lot', he continued. 'They don't get in the way much. Truth is we tell them what we want them to know and nothing more. They've very little grasp of what we really do.'

Warren tried unsuccessfully to disguise his dismay at this intelligence, but Arthur didn't notice. However he did manage to recover enough composure to continue lobbing questions at Arthur from his prepared list, even though he was beginning to wonder about the quality of the answers. But at least from the sound of things he could tell that his Lordship's absence was no great loss.

When asked how he found the right people to become trustees, Arthur had positively guffawed. 'We don't often have a vacancy as most of these duffers go on forever, bless 'em. If we do have a spare seat, because of a death or whatever, usually another trustee will have a friend or former colleague who'll be only too happy to stand in – someone from his old regiment, perhaps.'

'Truth is we tell them what we want them to know.'

What Arthur was saying confirmed what Warren had been reading that very morning on the train on his way to his visit with OSA, in a helpful book called *Over Goal* by Kay Sprinkel Grace (Emerson and Church, USA), an American author. Describing the arcane practices that often still inhabit voluntary organisations on both sides of the Atlantic, she had written:

'Those recruited in haste are often assured that there's "nothing to it" (being on the board). They are told such things as, "you don't have to do anything but come to

meetings"; or "we just need your name"; or (the worst), "we're desperate to submit a full slate of board nominees – please say yes".'

Warren began to realise that he might learn more from the OSA board about what not to do than what he should do. Whilst he felt that could, in a way, be useful, it certainly wasn't enjoyable, or a good use of time. He decided he'd heard enough and though Arthur seemed disappointed (he appeared set to go on for the rest of the day), Warren made his excuses, thanked his host politely and left, feeling a bit depressed. He hoped he wouldn't be as disappointed by the next board he was due to interview. He hoped that he would find it to be somewhat stronger and more independent.

Sadly, Warren was to be disappointed. But in rather a different way from that which he'd expected.

A strong board

Accompanied by three back-up staff all looking more than a little flustered, the Honourable Camilla ffoulkes-Lanningham, chair of trustees and Ron Huggins, executive director were arranged on the steps to meet Warren as his taxi turned into the drive of the imposing Regency mansion that houses the headquarters of the Safe Highways Trust, a road users' watchdog focusing on the rights and safety of the non-motorist. The driver brought his cab to rest just past the small knot of people who were gathered to meet Warren. In so doing he caused his passenger to witness a brief but clumsy exchange as the large lady in the bright red pashmina pushed the diminutive senior executive in his dapper pin-striped suit out of the way so she could be first to meet their visitor.

This was Camilla, the powerful, charismatic and much-feared chair of SHT. Warren stumbled from his taxi to be swept up by the imposing woman in red and propelled through the revolving front door before he knew what was happening.

Only later that evening did it dawn on Warren that, despite her title and airs and graces, the formidable Camilla isn't really of the aristocracy, though she aspires, with some success, to give the contrary impression. She isn't even really entitled to her double-barrelled name. The truth is, many years ago Camilla had married into 'old' money, so she is now able to rejoice in a life of ease financed by an elderly husband with declining capacities and a bank account so well-endowed that, for Camilla, paid work needn't be considered. This leaves her free to devote her time to a range of 'good works' designed to edge her further up the social ladder. Camilla, Warren realised, is the living embodiment of what the British call 'Lady Bountiful', a breed of well-meaning 'doer of good' found in one form or another in most countries around the globe.

Even before their meeting had started there was little doubt that the Honourable Camilla ffoulkes-Lanningham, chair of trustees at the Safe Highways Trust, would be doing most of the talking. Reflecting later on their roller coaster of an encounter, Warren fancied that no sooner had Ron, the director, said 'Hello, I'm Ron Huggins…' than

Camilla had interrupted, positively booming out her words, 'What Ron means is hello and welcome! Welcome to the Safe Highways Trust! We're so delighted you could...'

Then whisking her guest quickly inside, she'd dominated the conversation completely, almost without a pause for breath, for the next three hours.

Camilla did have some revealing insights to offer on the functioning of the board of trustees...

Warren couldn't actually remember Ron saying anything of substance all afternoon. However Warren tried to involve him, Camilla always talked for Ron. It quickly became clear that she tells him what to do as well.

Camilla did have some revealing insights to offer on the functionings of the board of trustees of the Safe Highways Trust. The previous week had witnessed an action-packed trustees' meeting, convened to consider some rather controversial proposals. These had been put before the board by two new (and therefore, evidently, inexperienced and easily misled) trustees, apparently egged on by some equally misguided former members of staff.

'We soon saw off that nonsense, didn't we Ronald?' said Camilla, though it was a statement rather than a question and Ron didn't even attempt to answer.

'Really', Camilla rolled on, 'SHT's policy on safety issues was laid down very firmly at the trustees' seminar nine years ago and we're not about to change that, whatever they or any other "lefties" may try to foist onto us.'

Warren gathered that these policy changes had been proposed following new research findings about the safety benefits of wearing high visibility clothing at night. A group of the staff had suggested that the Trust's ageing publications should be revised to take account of this.

'What's more', Camilla was now getting a bit heated, 'they knew very well we couldn't possibly have any budget for something like that. Of course we have to be safety conscious, but we can't do things if we don't have the budget. I mean, imagine the cost of reprinting all our publications.'

Warren mused quietly to himself that this might be rather the point, for an organisation committed to road safety, but Camilla shivered at the mere thought. Warren learned that to justify their rejection of the motion the board had apparently successfully discredited the research findings. This struck him at the time as more of an economy measure than a decision in the interests of safety, but he thought better of saying anything.

'And anyway', Camilla chuntered on oblivious to her audience's concern, 'if we hadn't nipped this subversion in the bud, next thing they'd be raking up that old nest of vipers about diversifying our fundraising sources...'

Camilla paused mid-sentence as if, self-evident though the lunacy of such a suggestion must be, her listeners would nevertheless appreciate time to digest the extent of its idiocy.

'Remember that, Ronnie?' She whacked Ron firmly in the ribs then sailed on regardless.

'Imagine this, Mr Maxwell. These staff had the effrontery to suggest that we trustees should help them with their fundraising efforts, even that some of us should be making big gifts ourselves. I said, we'll have no more of that sort of talk, thank you. Oh no. Our charity does very well from its government grant, little dribs and drabs of trust and foundation donations, that direct mail stuff, plus what we make from selling our books and maps and so on. We don't have to stand in the street with the begging bowl quite yet', she proclaimed, sitting back and folding her arms.

> '... even that some of us should be making big gifts ourselves.'

In an effort to steer Camilla away from the topic of rebellious and ungrateful senior staff, Warren then asked about meeting frequency and structure. Camilla was typically forthright. 'Well I can only get up to town on Thursdays so we have our meetings on the first Thursday of each month. I like to get the meeting over with in the morning so I can have the afternoon free for other important things I have to do whilst I'm in town.'

Warren suspected visiting her society friends might be high among those, but said nothing. He also resisted a question about trustee's expenses that had popped into his head unbidden.

Camilla continued, 'Most of our trustees, of course, are too old or too busy to attend every board meeting, but there's always three or four dependables at every session – mostly because they've got nothing else to do, poor dears. So it's not difficult to get a quorum you know, we only need four. And Major-General Smithers almost always turns up. He's a handful, that man, a bit too strong-minded for my liking. But he is thorough, as well as dogged, and keeps us on track if we're reviewing legislation, or complicated things like that.'

Ron smiled weakly at this. He considers Smithers a pompous, ill-tempered, ultra-sanctimonious old hypocrite, but as usual kept this view to himself.

Camilla hurried on in her brief review of the core competencies of the current SHT board, as if in describing their various insensitivities and intolerances she could convince her listener that all her board colleagues are as tough-minded and as strong as she is. 'Atkinson, our treasurer, like the poor, is always with us of course, and he could bore for England...'

Gingerly Warren interrupted this flow of useless information to ask about the minutes and whether he could see a copy of the minute book.

Camilla sat bolt upright as if electrocuted. 'Oh no', she said, pronouncing each word as if it were a sentence. 'I can't let you have the minutes, they're strictly confidential. Even the staff don't get to see those, you know.

'Why, I remember a few years back when we were interviewing for a new executive director', she shot a meaningful sidelong glance at Ron, who shifted in his seat uneasily, 'there was this candidate – a big, pushy, nosey man, full of prying questions. He wanted to see the minutes of our board meetings and a whole lot of other internal documents before he would consider coming back for a second interview. Some of the other trustees were quite keen on him so suggested we go along with it. Not on your nelly, I said. They soon agreed with me. They usually do you know.

'We're a very united board. I always say there are just two ways things are done here, our way and the wrong way. And we soon sort out anyone who disagrees with our decisions, so there's just one way things are done around here...'

This story seemed likely to run and run, but fortunately at that moment a group of about six employees swept into the meeting room, seemingly in great consternation at finding it already occupied. Ron flapped off to sort things out, leaving Warren alone with Camilla.

'Tell me about how you assess the board's performance', Warren asked in an effort to change the subject. Camilla looked confused.

'I... er... we... well, we don't do that here you know, there wouldn't be much point, would there? I mean, it would be better to assess the management's performance, don't you think? They're the ones who have to do what we tell them, aren't they? What on earth do you mean, assess the board's performance?'

Warren felt the need of a subject change again. He'd wanted to ask her what she saw as the board's main roles, but he thought better of it. So instead he asked, hoping this wouldn't be too challenging for Camilla, who clearly ruled with a rod of iron, 'Umm… how do you go about recruiting new board members?'

'Oh, good question', responded Camilla, as if surprised. 'Well of course, if I know the candidate personally then that's all right, there's no need to go to any trouble. But if I don't – and sometimes someone is put forward that I really haven't heard of beforehand – well, then we go through a very thorough selection process, very thorough. I ask Ron to brief them fully on the Trust and what we are doing. He can do that reasonably well, I suppose.'

'I ask him to leave the room if we come to anything confidential.'

She didn't look convinced, but rolled on. 'Then I get Mr Atkinson to take them through the accounts and go over what a trustee's duties are. That sorts out most of them, believe me. If they survive that they'll survive most things I can tell you. Then I interview them myself for several hours, with Ron of course. Though', and here

Camilla seemed to be almost reflecting to herself, 'I do ask him to leave the room if we come to anything confidential.

'After that, if I like the new trustee and he seems the right type, we'll appoint him. But I do turn down a lot, even at that stage you know.' Camilla laughed, 'You should see the surprise on their faces Mr Maxwell. Most of them think that because they're volunteering, I mean unpaid, it never occurs to them that we might actually turn them down.'

Warren glanced at the lengthy list of trustees in the annual report Camilla had given him. From their names alone he could tell that they were all from the English middle-to-upper-class conservative establishment. Noting this absence of diversity, Warren thought that probably most organisations get the trustees and trustee board that they deserve. He very politely thanked Camilla for her time and got up to leave.

Just then Ron re-entered the room. It seems he'd just survived a stressful encounter with several of his senior managers, who some weeks previously had booked the meeting room for this time and apparently resented being forced at short notice to find something less suitable elsewhere, because the meeting room had been commandeered just that morning by the chair of trustees.

Camilla seemed genuinely perplexed, 'Why on earth should they be upset? I am the chair of trustees…'

Warren overheard this exchange just as he was halfway back into the revolving front door. He gave the heavy door a firm shove and in response the swing of the door propelled him into the cool, clear air beyond.

Later that day Warren received a phone call from a very apologetic Ron Huggins. It seemed Warren had chosen rather a bad day for his visit, as that very morning Camilla, chair of trustees, had informed Ron of the board's decision to cancel all donor acquisition initiatives for the rest of the year. This, Ron went on to explain, was just the latest in a long line of sweeping, irrational and largely incompetent decisions that had been handed down to him by his domineering, overbearing board. So, along with most of what remained of his management team, Ron was forced to consider resignation. This was the last straw, he said. He was going to throw in the towel and head off to calmer pastures.

But, Warren realised, Ron hadn't quite worked up the courage to tell Camilla about this. Not yet.

A change of luck

Although very different from each other, both of the organisations Warren has visited so far have been equally disappointing to him. Apart from some fairly obvious lessons in how not to lead a volunteer board, Warren really hasn't picked up any hints or tips he could use, or good ideas that he could borrow. He is none the wiser as to what he should be looking to introduce at FuturePoint to make his board a model of good practice. He hopes that he's just been unlucky and that he'll learn what really matters from his next and final visit.

A balanced board

Warren paused outside the unassuming offices of his third assignment, the Committee for Limiting Climate Change, or CLiCC as it is better known. He hoped that they would click with him, too.

Serena Rani, the chief executive, collected Warren from the brightly lit, well laid-out reception area and led him directly up to the boardroom, where she introduced him to the chair of trustees, David Prescott. As he entered Warren noted that the room seemed just right for a serious nonprofit organisation: comfortable and well-appointed, but in no way ostentatious. An appealing presentation of the charity's work decorated the far wall, displayed around two truly stunning photographs of pristine, unpolluted rural scenes. Some appetising-looking sandwiches and fruit had been set out for lunch near where a small group of chairs had been arranged in an intimate circle away from the large boardroom table, near to the door. He shook hands with a friendly, relaxed looking businessman of about his own age. This was David Prescott.

'We've allocated an hour for this discussion', said Serena, who as with David, Warren took an immediate liking to. 'But if you are able to stay longer, why don't you come to our trustees' meeting after lunch and sit in as an observer, as our guest? Then you can see for yourself how our board works.'

Warren nodded in assent, gratefully. As David Prescott poured the tea, they settled down to their meeting. The visitor kicked off by asking both of his hosts for their general overview of the CLiCC board.

Getting the thinking right

'A volunteer board can easily become a liability to an organisation rather than an asset', said David. 'We have to work hard to ensure that we are always adding value and are not a burden on our cause. This means we have to get our thinking right first.

'Three years ago', he explained, 'my predecessor

thoroughly reviewed the board, its achievements and its structure. Trustees were assessed both individually and as a team. It was an indispensable experience and led to some major rethinking, followed by a substantial restructuring.

'We often have to work hard on our board members, both individually and collectively, to do our utmost to ensure board unity and buy-in. And we don't expect perfection, or even ask for it. Our board is a broad church, with members who enjoy varying degrees of comfort. But overall, everyone believes in the strategy and commits him or herself to it totally. If anyone didn't, we'd go to great lengths to try to resolve whatever were the issues, but if that proved impossible then he or she would have to go elsewhere.

'Our role is to support the management, to make their jobs easier...'

'Our role is to support the management, to make their jobs easier and to ensure the charity delivers on all its obligations. If we can't support the management – who we appointed – then it's our duty to replace them as quickly as possible with people we can support. We have no room for petty squabbles or disunity.'

Warren was impressed, and settled in to enjoying his tea and the conversation. He asked some general questions about the duties and responsibilities of trustees.

Trustees' responsibilities

'There's a number of helpful sources of information on such things', explained David. 'If you like I'll give you a list, before you go.'

Warren was delighted. This meeting was already paying dividends. (The list the chairman gave him can be found on pages 70 and 71.)

'Being a trustee carries several specific responsibilities', David continued, 'and these must be made clear to all new trustees, with reminders from time to time for older hands. We're lucky in this country, our Charity Commission provides a free, easy-to-read guide for all new trustees called *The Essential Trustee: What You Need to Know*. We give a copy to all candidates applying to join our board.

'In North America there's an organisation called BoardSource that provides similar publications and other resources. They have a helpful list called *Ten Basic Responsibilities of Nonprofit Boards*. That's worth getting too. They also provide sample job descriptions for different board members, which many find helpful, and information on how to find a specialist consultant and lots of other practical stuff.'

'It can seem daunting at first', Serena chipped in sympathetically, 'but really in a well-run organisation the responsibilities of a trustee are not too arduous, because the practical management tasks are all delegated to appropriately qualified and competent senior staff.

'Trustees have a duty of care and are required to ensure that the charity is well run and always operates within the law. But provided they act prudently and responsibly and exercise reasonable care and skill when making decisions – and of course these are the qualities they were recruited for – then they need have few worries.'

Reassured by this, Warren then wanted to know what was required in terms of frequency, length and type of meetings.

David laughed, 'There are no rules really. As with size and composition of the board, these are matters for each board to decide, based on their individual circumstances and needs.'

Here Serena mildly reprimanded her chairman. 'Well, we might like to think there are no rules, but actually we are restricted by our status as a charitable company limited by guarantee. This means that, like any company in the UK, we have to have a "memorandum and articles of association", which sets out our rules on subjects that include frequency of meetings, what constitutes a quorum, appointment of officers, etc.

'At CLiCC we have our procedures set out in our governing document, but that's been constructed – and recently updated – to take account of the kind of organisation we want to be.'

'You're quite right', said David. 'Any registered charity will have a governing document and though trustees usually reserve the right to change it if necessary, there are rules on how they can do this.

You do have to keep proper minutes, of course, and to record formally that the duties of the trustees have been properly discharged.

'Similarly there are no hard and fast rules about officers of the board. A chairperson is normal...'

'And would be rather hard to do without', interjected Serena.

David continued unfazed, 'Equally I can't imagine how we'd function without a treasurer', he said looking suddenly rather serious, 'and, because I sometimes can't make meetings, we recently appointed a vice-chair, which has made my life much easier.'

Serena then asked Warren if it would be helpful to go through the practical steps that lead up to each board meeting and he leapt at the opportunity.

'I try always to meet up with the chairman a week to ten days before each meeting', she explained, 'to clarify our objectives and agree both the agenda and the strategy for the meeting itself. This time is necessary to get the board papers together and sent out well before the actual meeting, so all trustees have ample time to read and prepare, or at least have no excuse for not doing so.

'Sometimes, for various reasons, we can only manage to get together over the phone, but face-to-face is best. This planning is crucial. We always have a packed agenda and a need for brisk time management if trustees are to get the information they need, plus enough opportunity to discuss and debate key issues. So we separate agenda items into those that are for information and those that require decisions. We like to ensure there are no surprises. "No surprises" is a bit of a catch-phrase of ours', Serena said, turning to David with a smile.

'My job', David volunteered, 'is highly unenviable.' He seemed so cheerful Warren assumed he wasn't entirely serious. 'I have to allow enough space for proper discussion, but also need to be firm enough to shut people up and move the debate on. At times it's a bit like herding cats. But our trustees are good people and all understand what needs to be done. Plus of course they appreciate a well-run meeting and being able to get away on time, with all business done. Often I'll call them individually a couple of days before, to clear any potential stumbling blocks in advance.

'At times it's a bit like herding cats.'

'Serena is right when she says there should be no surprises. But I also try to include a few things on the agenda that will intrigue or excite trustees, so they can anticipate an interesting and enjoyable meeting. It's important that meetings should always be rewarding and enjoyable. If they are not people won't come, or if they do they won't be in a very good mood. So we place high emphasis on refreshing our trustees' sense of the mission and ensuring that the meetings are both interesting and fun.

'We make sure all trustees have the chance to visit

our projects to see for themselves the work we do and to meet our staff. This helps everyone to appreciate the extra value that the board adds. It's invaluable for refreshing trustees' commitment and good for staff too.'

Warren thought all this sounded like eminent good sense.

David went on to explain that at each board meeting he arranges for at least one trustee freshly returned from a project to tell a short but instructive, even moving story describing CLiCC's work and the people, animals, or ecosystems it helps. 'It's a priceless way of focusing the whole board's attention on our mission and why we do what we do,' he explained. 'And it hones their storytelling skills too.'

What the board is for

'You know, this seems a really silly question', said Warren, 'but it's something that occurred to me a while ago. In most commercial businesses there is just one top management group, the senior executives, perhaps supported by one or two non-executive directors, who collectively form "the board".

'In a charity there are two very distinct teams, the senior management and the volunteer board of trustees. And they don't overlap. So, assuming they have appointed a competent management group, just what is the trustee board for?'

'It's a good question', replied David, 'one that

perhaps more nonprofit boards and organisations should ask of themselves. Too few charities, it seems to me, have a clear understanding of the different but complementary roles of senior management and trustees. Most of their problems arise from their failure to clarify and comprehend these roles.

'The real breakthrough for our board was agreeing precisely what is the board's role and what isn't. Then working to make sure that all members of our board know their individual roles within that and how collectively and individually our roles differ from those of the staff management team. The single most important realisation for an effective volunteer board is to understand that the board's role is governance and the management team's role is to manage the organisation.

'The real break-through for our board was agreeing precisely what is the board's role and what isn't.'

'In my view, having an outside "expert" board of active and committed individuals can be of great value to any nonprofit or voluntary organisation. Individual volunteers are willing to serve in this role because they believe in the cause and can see that the gift of their time and experience is the best way they can help a worthwhile organisation achieve its important mission. But they must focus on where they add value and what their role and relationships with the rest of the organisation are, or should be, ideally. If they work together successfully, the right group of volunteers can become a board that will make a good organisation great.

'Trustees', David stressed, 'should understand that they have a duty to challenge the status quo and if need be to ask awkward questions. All boards benefit if at least one member is what my friend David Carrington, in his article *Board Membership with Purpose and Fun*, refers to as "a pleasant irritant" – someone who will force the board to think a little differently.'

Here he rummaged among some papers in his bag and handed Warren a well-thumbed document. 'Read this', he advised. Readers can download this useful article in full at www.whitelionpress.com

Proving value

Warren enquired whether the CLiCC board had ever submitted itself to formal evaluation. David's response was that such evaluation at regular intervals is essential to help the board to focus and improve and to prove that it adds value to the organisation.

David explained that, while each board may have different ideas, objectives and systems for board evaluation, he believes it is important that the board is assessed formally, at least in part, by external assessors and that the outcomes and lessons should be widely published. CLiCC's evaluation process is fully described in what he calls *The Trustees' Handbook*, a loose-leaf guide covering all aspects of the charity's governance that is given to every new trustee. Warren thought this a great idea and noted down in his book: *'must have one'.*

As their discussion progressed, Serena and David between them passed round the sandwiches and the fruit juice. Warren thought that lunch tasted as good as it looked and recorded in his notebook, 'to improve morale, make sure FuturePoint's sandwich lunches are *much* better'.

Key people, key committees

David's response to Warren's question (between mouthfuls) about committees was surprising. 'Simply as a way of spreading the load and ensuring that all the board's work is done, some subcommittees will be unavoidable. But I suggest these are kept to an absolute minimum and are never used as a means of deflecting issues that the whole board should deal with to a smaller "inner circle" of elite trustees.

'The UK fundraising expert Alan Clayton once said that committees get in the way of dreams and I think that's too often true. We all know the saying, "a camel is a horse designed by a committee".

'Committees can too easily be a barrier, can stifle ideas or institutionalise objections to good ideas. So at CLiCC we only have committees to perform essential functions that otherwise would make full board meetings too cumbersome. For some needs we do create time-limited working groups, though. We use these for specific tasks that we want to deal with quickly, where we are clear that the work involved must be completed within a defined time.'

David continued, 'Currently we have just three committees: audit, investment and board development. Other similar organisations often also have research and policy development committees, but we've decided to deal with these issues within the main board.

'The audit and investment committees are both specialist financial functions with crystal clear remits. "Audit" ensures that our accounts are formally audited in all centres and deals with any questions that arise from the accounts before they are published. "Investment" oversees the deployment of any surplus funds, though we keep these to a minimum, and ensures all our financial resources are put to the best possible use. Trustees with a senior business background usually make up these committees, though from time to time we draw in non-trustees with specialist experience. Both of these are chaired by the honorary treasurer.

'Some subcommittees will be unavoidable... but should be kept to a minimum.'

'The board development committee', David went on, 'is mainly concerned with succession planning.

It's chaired by the chairman of the main board and led by the CEO. This group researches, identifies, selects and interviews potential new trustees for proposal to the full board and also prepares and oversees induction and development plans for each trustee, while monitoring their service agreement and retirement date. It's probably the most important of all the board's subcommittees.'

Don't neglect retired trustees

'Regarding retired trustees', said David ruefully, 'it's a sad fact, but most nonprofits don't make any effort to keep in touch with former trustees after they've retired. For the recently retired trustee who has just completed six or more years working at the heart of an important organisation, the sense of lost interest and lost status on having to step down can be profound.

'Of course each of our trustees knows the rules when he or she joins so leaving at the end of term comes as no surprise. But however prepared a trustee might be, the day when his or her trusteeship comes to its inevitable end can still be a considerable upheaval. It takes time for most people to adjust. Former trustees often tell us they suffer a sense of loss and disconnection when they make the transition from important trustee one minute to just another supporter the next.

'To avoid the worst aspects of this, CLiCC is in the process of setting up a special group of former trustees and former staff too, to explore ways that these important and experienced people can continue to contribute to the organisation that they so love. Called "friends in high places", the group will be informal and initially its tasks and objectives won't be time-consuming or daunting. But its potential could be considerable. All that's needed is some creativity, optimism and a modicum of commitment to this very talented and valuable group of supporters, who almost certainly will want to find ways to continue their involvement, either by giving their time, or in some other way.'

Serena interjected with another idea that Warren immediately wrote in his book. 'We also offer departing trustees a departure interview. This is an opportunity for the trustee to say his or her piece on leaving and be valued for it. Both positives and negatives come out in these interviews, so they're highly instructive.'

Trustees as donors – and a bonus idea

Serena then went on to say, 'Like most voluntary organisations, CLiCC depends on its donors. Few things are more important to a nonprofit's success in donor development than the understanding and wholehearted support of its board. It's more likely that you'll be given that support if your board members all personally identify with your donors, particularly through being donors themselves.

'As well as most of them being donors themselves', ventured Serena, looking more than a little pleased with herself, 'all of our trustees are encouraged to leave a legacy to our organisation too. We don't believe that just because someone gives us their time they can't – and won't want to – also give to us financially. Many of the charity's volunteers are also enthusiastic donors and that's true of our board too. As always though, giving of either time or money remains voluntary. We don't pressurise our trustees into giving, as we don't pressurise our donors.'

Serena then went on to outline a new innovation at CLiCC, which, again, Warren hurried to write down in his book.

'As a way of encouraging the board to align themselves closely with donors and beneficiaries we have, through the chairman, introduced the concept of an imaginary guest or guests at our board table. The idea is that no board meeting should take place without the realisation that there are lots of other individuals or groups who are intimately involved in and affected by the deliberations at our board table, but who can't be there personally for a variety of reasons. One such group is our beneficiaries. Another is certainly our donors. There may be others, but for us these are the most important.

'To ensure that the views and interests of our key "absent audiences" are never overlooked we create two empty places at our board table. We give the absent guest water, pad and pencil like any other attendee and place an empty chair where he or she would sit. This symbolism is powerful and impossible for board members to put to the backs of their minds. If space is limited, or just for variety, we sometimes dispense with the chair and other physical paraphernalia. But we don't let our board forget that there are real, important people waiting just outside the door of our boardroom, whose lives and potential our collective decisions will affect so deeply.'

'This symbolism is powerful and impossible for board members to put to the backs of their minds.'

'The "guest at table" idea is good practice in several ways', David added. 'It shows humility, and accountability. It encourages a positive piece of ritual. But mostly it reminds the board of the constant need to see their proceedings, behaviour and decisions through the eyes of their key constituencies, the people who are most affected by what they say and do.'

A final question

Realising that his time was nearly up, Warren quickly asked, 'How do you ensure that things don't go wrong?'

'In all things, Warren, the buck stops with the board', David said, looking very serious. 'But', and his smile returned, 'in practice we're not routinely concerned about things going wrong as management is charged with running the day-to-day affairs of the charity and we have great confidence in our management team. We work closely with them to agree a strategy and to review its implementation and relevance at sensible intervals. In their daily business the management team should know what has to come before the board, when and in what form.

'If the management team is as good as we believe it to be, things won't go wrong very often. When they do, Serena as CEO and her team know exactly when and about what to inform the trustees, should that be necessary. So we deal with any problems together as they arise. Because we're a fairly large, complex organisation and as a volunteer with limited time I can't possibly know all that's going on at any one time, Serena's intuitive understanding of what I need to know is the key component of our effective chair and CEO relationship. It's built on trust, because no other option would be viable.'

Serena took over, 'The only real assets a nonprofit organisation has are its reputation and "brand". So it's essential that trustees should be involved in anything that affects either of those things.

'At CLiCC we make sure that they are. We have guidelines prepared in advance to cover any situation that's likely to occur, for example, when we are campaigning on issues that might be controversial or in the public eye. So trustees are informed well in advance if, say, information might appear in the press. Really, the best safeguards are trust, openness and common sense.'

The clock had moved round, so Warren resisted the temptation to slip in one last question about the ideal level of funds to keep in reserves. But, as if by intuition, Serena dealt with this as a follow-up to her last observation about assets.

'We place great emphasis on managing our finances so we can always be sure to meet our obligations. But we don't believe in tying up our donors' funds in investments beyond the minimum essential for a reasonable level of security. The only exception has been buying this office, which in real terms over the years has proved better than paying rent. But other than this we don't have investments on the financial markets, because we'd rather use donors' funds for our mission, or to strengthen our fundraising capacity. Our board supports this wholeheartedly, as do our donors.'

'... we'd rather use our donors' funds for our mission...'

David then leaned forward towards Warren and said, 'We'll give you something before you go', he almost whispered, sounding very conspiratorial, 'that I think you will find priceless in your quest to build an effective volunteer board. It's our paper called *The 21 key aspects of good governance*, which we drafted after our trustees' "away day" seminar last year.'

Serena smiled and handed Warren a neatly typed information sheet. 'I had it ready for you', she said. 'But don't automatically adopt all it says, Warren. Rather, you should seek to adapt it to suit your organisation's needs.'

Warren smiled in grateful acceptance. 'This board', he thought, 'is the one I want to learn from and to be like.'

At that point other people began to drift into the room. Warren looked at the clock. There were about 20 minutes to go before the scheduled start of the trustees' meeting. As he finished his fruit juice he was introduced to many of the trustees, senior management team and invited guests who had all come, promptly, for the trustees' meeting. Warren noticed that while the atmosphere was very friendly and informal, everyone was punctual and smartly turned out. 'As it should be', he said to himself.

At the appointed hour, precisely on time, the trustees' meeting started. For the next three hours Warren was engrossed, so wrapped up in the affairs of this board that he felt fully a part of it. At one point he even interjected – politely through the chair of course – with a comment the relevance of which somewhat surprised him. The chairman thanked him, warmly. Warren glowed.

After the meeting had ended Warren started to take his leave. Grasping his notes and his copy of the 21 keys, plus CLiCC's brilliant annual report, its interesting-looking newsletter and a copy of its handbook for trustees, Warren thanked his hosts perhaps a little too profusely and shook hands a little too vigorously, apologising for the time he'd taken up. David and Serena assured him that if he'd learned anything from the meeting then, for them, it had been time well spent.

'Oh yes', thought Warren as he headed off to catch his train. 'I have indeed learned rather a lot from this meeting.'

Sitting back in his carriage on the train home, Warren settled down to read the paper on effective governance that he had been given by his generous hosts. As he began to read he couldn't help but notice the young woman to his left who was attempting, without much subtlety, to read the paper over his shoulder.

Though this was distracting at first, Warren soon became fully absorbed in his document and his dark-haired, nosey neighbour was soon pushed from mind by the pearls of wisdom on those two closely typed pages.

As he read, Warren added notes, conclusions and observations of his own to the list. These jottings, augmented by some of the lessons he learned later, are included here with the original 21 keys.

The 21 key aspects of good governance

1. The board serves the organisation, not the organisation serves the board.

Too many trustee boards have yet to open themselves up to the currently accepted standards and best practices of good governance, but the concept has spread widely recently and is gathering momentum in nonprofit organisations the world over. A healthy competition now holds sway in some boards that wish to show their organisations and the outside world that they are paragons of best practice. The nonprofit board Oscars can't be far off, and perhaps that would be no bad thing.

High among the indicators of good governance is an absence of pride and pomposity, combined with the realisation that the board is not the top layer of the organisation, it's just another vital but equal component that must fulfil its role effectively and deliver demonstrable value just like any other part. The board is no place for passengers, autocrats, or petty dictators. The board is there to serve.

2. Make sure everyone fully understands the different roles of the board and the

management 'top team'. *Management* **manages. The** *board* **governs. Define the different roles, making clear what governance means.**

The board deals with strategy, management deals with operations. Management proposes, the board approves – or not. So boards will mostly prove to be effective when they are questioning rather than answering.

Any board unable to leave the role of management to the full-time professionals it has appointed to run the organisation is not an effective board. If the CEO hasn't got the board's full confidence he or she should be required to improve or leave (or in exceptional circumstances the board or a part of it should leave). The CEO – with the board's help by all means – should appoint the senior management team. After all, it's the CEO's job to make the senior team deliver its objectives. No CEO can be reasonably expected to do this unless he or she has appointed the top management team himself/herself.

3. Agree the board's main roles. There are (usually) five.

• Watchdog: guardians of public interest, particularly for donors, beneficiaries and other stakeholders. Guardians of the brand, and reputation.

• Strategic planning (role shared with management) and formal approval and adoption of the strategy.

• Appoint, monitor and if necessary remove the CEO. Approve his/her appointment of management team, assisting as required.

• Support for management and, through them, the staff, to help them do their jobs better and to ensure the organisation succeeds.

• Understand the finances of the organisation, read and (having understood them) approve the accounts. Trustees are also required to ensure that their organisation is fully open and accountable in providing a complete and detailed description of what the organisation has done with the money it has raised.

There are exceptions to the above, but not many. Volunteer boards can take on additional roles if the management team wishes them to although, given the time pressures under which most board members operate, additional tasks may be unwise as they may dilute the board's effectiveness at its core functions.

These five, properly discharged, are the key roles that make voluntary boards such beacons of good governance and such an exceptional asset to their organisations. All new trustees should be made aware of these and every so often all established trustees should be required, on a scale of one to five, to evaluate themselves and their board against them.

Different countries may have differing rules or guidelines for nonprofit boards so it pays to familiarise yourself with whatever laws, best practice, or guidance govern the board's role and responsibilities in your country.

4. Prepare a written strategy, together with the CEO, just covering the board and what it does, that everyone can buy into, board members and senior staff alike.

There are few hard and fast rules on board strategies. The strategy document can be slim or fat as tastes and circumstances dictate. It's probably a good idea to review it from time to time – it can be updated or replaced each year, or it can run unchanged for years.

The board's strategy should fit in snugly with the organisation's overall strategy. And it'll have full buy-in if it's produced jointly with the management team rather than handed down to them from on high. It'll help if it's in plain language, stripped of pomposity and jargon and no longer than it needs to be.

It is important to know to whom the board is

accountable. Many countries have legislation and established regulatory mechanisms that cover this. Those that don't will depend on a document or charter that establishes the board's responsibilities and parameters, such as a memorandum of understanding, or articles of association. Boards often have many stakeholders and it is important that these have clear access to what the board is doing and ways of ensuring it is appropriately accountable.

5. Keep the CEO involved (and management team too). Never meet without the CEO, unless in a crisis that involves replacing the CEO.

Traditionally boards love to be secretive and frequently gather behind closed doors. While some circumstances necessitate confidentiality, most of a board's business doesn't need to be secret so should be conducted openly and transparently. A good board has a duty to share its processes and outcomes not just with management and other staff but with supporters and other interested audiences too.

6. Immerse all board members in the board's mission. Let trustees see the work personally, for themselves.

Your board members need to fully understand

the work of the organisation they are to govern. This means that there is no substitute for experiencing it themselves, in person. The nature of the work that your organisation does means this will be easier for some organisations than for others. But it is almost always worthwhile and should be seen as an essential part of good governance.

7. Work with the management team to produce a rolling organisational strategy. Ensure there is universal commitment to this strategy, 'the glue that binds us together'.

Facilitating and approving the organisation's strategy and the process that produces it is one of the most important of the board's roles. For the strategy to work, it's essential that the whole organisation is involved in its drafting and that the process is fair, transparent and well-managed.

8. Reduce paperwork. Make sure your meetings serve the needs of the organisation, not those of the trustees.

Most boards produce too much paper, which is an unnecessary burden not just for the trustees and others who have to wade through it all but, perhaps more importantly, for the usually hard-pressed staff who have to prepare it and often spend weeks and even months in the task.

A minimum level of paperwork is desirable and necessary and it is the board's task not to set that level but to work with the senior management team to ensure it has the paperwork it needs, but no more.

9. Get the board's balance right: introduce formal terms of service, retirement policy, age and gender balance, representation from the field, regions, retaining institutional memory, etc.

Achieving a balanced board is important, not just in terms of its physical composition in background and demographics but also in its personality, its skills sets, and even its interests and attitudes. Creating an appropriate balance is an ongoing challenge, a work that is never quite complete.

While diversity and balance are great board strengths, nevertheless in some areas the board has to be united, consistent and absolutely of one mind. This includes its members' commitment to the mission and aims of their organisation, their vision of the future for their organisation and their belief in and commitment to the job they all do, collectively, as the board of trustees.

10. Establish a board development committee, or group to continuously recruit the right skills and experience for a qualified, balanced and representative board. Its roles include identifying and recruiting trustees, induction, development and goal-setting. Produce an excellent board recruitment pack.

Develop a skills matrix and retirement schedule. Train the chair and CEO in recruitment skills.

No trustee should feel he or she has a job for life. Ideally boards should opt for a regular turnover of trustees – most decide on either two or three periods of three years after which most trustees will leave. Only in exceptional circumstances should a trustee be reappointed, and even then a 'fallow' year off the board should be mandatory. He or she should return for no more than three years, probably less. This means that a regular programme of identification and recruitment of suitable candidates will be essential. This is a huge and very important task, best undertaken by a small subgroup of competent and hard-working trustees and senior managers who can make sure that sufficient candidates of the right calibre and personality are brought forward and effectively screened, approved by the full board, appointed and developed.

Your own judgement will tell you what should go in the board recruitment pack, but while including all the essentials (such as the trustees' handbook and the annual report) it's best to keep it short, focused and interesting.

11. Offer frequent development opportunities for board members so that they can grow in their roles, increase the value of their contribution and avoid becoming stale. Implement a regular induction programme for new trustees, which established members can join too, for refreshment and renewal.

Many organisations combine the development role with induction, so that immersion in the work of their nonprofit is an ongoing process for board members. Make induction fun as well as instructive. But respect the time your volunteers are giving up for this. So make it effective, informative and enjoyable.

12. Run good, interesting and enjoyable meetings. Make sure they start and end on time.

Being a trustee is far from all about meetings, but the meetings can be the focal point for board members and it's important that they be as good and as effective as possible.

13. Communicate effectively: between meetings, to staff, to the outside world, but mostly to the board to let them know any important happenings.

Little and often is probably a good rule here, but use your knowledge of each individual trustee to ensure it's the right amount and not too frequent or too scarce.

14. Practise openness and accountability. Publish your governance procedures and outcomes widely.

Publish the board's minutes of meetings to all stakeholders, edited only for the genuinely confidential. Allowing other staff and visitors to attend board meetings and to present to board meetings will spread unity and dispel mystery. Don't usher visitors out immediately once they've completed their part of the agenda. Let the world see what your board does and how it functions. Everyone will almost certainly be impressed, and reassured.

Put your trustees' handbook on your website and offer it through your annual report.

15. Establish procedures for managing tasks/committees.

All boards have subcommittees it seems and

although some are essential to the smooth running of the board, many have more than they need. It's often a better idea to form a working group with a fixed task and deadline rather than a committee whose existence is enshrined into perpetuity. Whatever committee functions are right for your board, it is crucial to avoid the possibility of any committee expropriating the essential functions of the whole board. No committee should be able to make any trustee feel excluded from what he or she needs to properly discharge their responsibilities as a trustee. Minutes of subcommittee meetings should be included with board papers.

16. Ensure that when board members work for the organisation in addition to their trustee role, both inside and outside the board, that they do so as respected volunteers, not revered and unchallengeable trustees.

Too often trustees become an elite power, which can be very disruptive particularly to staff. The best way round this is to ensure that they have dual status as both board member and volunteer. Then to gently deflate any notions of superiority that may surround the role of board member.

In most cultures it is the board collectively that is

the legal entity and has the clearly defined role and responsibility, rather than its individual members. It is useful to stress to board members that they work for and support the organisation collectively in a statutory role, but individually in an advisory role.

17. Conduct regular formal board assessment.

Just like any other part of the organisation, the board of trustees has to be assessed regularly, openly and professionally. As each board is different this can take many forms and be as structured or informal as seems appropriate. A sample structure for a board evaluation can be found on the publisher's website, www.whitelionpress.com

18. Organise board retreats regularly (this can be dispensed with if your board meetings involve an overnight stay for all trustees).

In addition to whatever is on the agenda, their value is in the social interactions between board members. This is where bonds are formed and team spirit is built. Joint visits to see the work in practice help this too.

19. Have strategies for dealing with difficult board members.

All boards suffer from this some time or other. Inevitably there will be one, or more, difficult member who will disrupt the team and cause rather than resolve problems. The key is not to try to ignore them in the hope that they will go away. Almost invariably, they won't. Boards – or perhaps more commonly, board chairs – need to be firm, clear and fair with trustees who are not performing as agreed, including both those who don't turn up to meetings and those who persistently try to hog the limelight. Obviously any failing trustee should be quickly removed so as to create space for another who will contribute.

20. Retain a sense of humour, celebrate successes and have fun.

It's been said that humour isn't an absolute essential, but many experienced trustees disagree. No board will function as well as it might without the enjoyment of a balanced amount of humour and an appropriate dose of fun. This isn't a tiny thing either – it's rather fundamental.

Yet some boards take themselves so seriously that being with them is almost like being at a funeral; their meetings are like church services and when the chair speaks it seems he's making a speech or delivering a sermon. Long faces and solemnity don't facilitate good decisions or lead to inspirational ideas or good governance. Boards need to be serious, of course, but not taking oneself too seriously is just as important as being serious enough. An enjoyable, light atmosphere can mitigate any excesses. It's worth making provision for it.

And it goes without saying that trustees should visibly celebrate their own and their organisation's successes – while not putting themselves centre stage, of course.

21. Share your experience and knowledge freely with other boards and trustees.

One of the greatest assets of the nonprofit sector is the openness and spirit of freely sharing information, experience and results that characterises voluntary organisations. While taking full advantage of this, trustees should in turn commit themselves and their organisation to open and generous sharing with others.

Brief encounter/close encounters

Warren sighed contentedly as he finished absorbing the list of 21 keys. He reflected on how valuable and informative the three visits he had undertaken had been to him and to his charity, FuturePoint, in showing what FuturePoint's board might aspire to, and what it should avoid. 'This list', he thought to himself, 'is gold. Pure gold.'

The young woman to his left saw her opportunity

and leapt in. Somewhat ruefully Warren realised that, like it or not, for the next hour or so until he reached his destination, he had a conversation companion.

But it turned out that the young woman's interest had been piqued not by the debonair Warren himself, but by what he was reading. By the wildest of chances it transpired that this young person was, indeed still is, Theresa Greene, head of finance at ActionRights, one of Britain's largest development charities. She told Warren that she had been working closely with her CEO and board chair on a project to restructure and revitalise their international board of trustees. The next hour flashed past as Theresa regaled Warren with ActionRights' experiences in board development and Warren filled page after page of his by now burgeoning notebook.

Theresa was most helpful on the subject of recruiting new board members: she told Warren that it is an apparently endless

She introduced him to the concept of 'the three Ts' ...

challenge for today's nonprofit board. She introduced him to the concept of 'the three Ts', which stand for time, talent and treasure. 'This phrase', said Theresa, 'is frequently quoted in American nonprofits as summarising *the* essential qualities for a new trustee – what you need to bring with you if you want to join the board or, conversely, what your board needs to find in its new recruits.'

Theresa went on to explain that the concept of 'treasure' might not seem quite appropriate in some cultures where board members are not expected to contribute financially to their charity, nor to help with fundraising. But that expectation is changing, slowly perhaps, but almost everywhere. Before long it will be assumed that board members are required, within the limits of their financial means, to contribute to the organisation that they govern.

As Theresa put it, 'This isn't just a token of their commitment to the organisation, it's also to encourage others. How can an organisation solicit major gifts from donors if its own leadership has not shown the way?'

Warren nodded sagely in agreement, but at the same time thinking that the board at FuturePoint would never buy it.

'The other two Ts', continued the confident Theresa, 'unquestionably apply universally, although in our experience I'd add a fourth crucial requisite, commitment – although I suppose that will spoil things as it doesn't start with a T.'

Theresa laughed, then regained her serious tone. 'Whatever, finding people with these qualities and any additional specifics your board might require is not easy.'

The ActionRights experience

Warren continued to nod sagely. Theresa now had his undivided attention, and rose to the occasion.

'Recruiting new trustees is perhaps the most important and difficult task facing any board chair. At ActionRights it's very much a work in progress, so not something at which anyone on the board or the management team considers themselves as expert.

'Early on ActionRights realised the value of an effective board development committee. Superficially its role seems straightforward – identifying potential new recruits to the board and developing their contribution once they've passed the selection process.' Warren thought this sounded easy enough, but was told to consider the following.

• Until recently ActionRights' board was fairly typical of the stereotype UK board – mainly male, British and middle class. There was no practical limit on a trustee's length of service and people did serve on the board for many years. ActionRights now asks trustees to serve for up to two consecutive terms of three years after which they must retire. They can only return after a gap of at least a year and then only as an exception. A regular exception to this however is the board chair, who is usually required to serve at least three years after appointment, irrespective of previous service.

• The board has 15 members, which ActionRights considers optimum – the constitution states a minimum of 10. Statistically ActionRights will need to find two or three new trustees each year from now on just to maintain the current board.

• In addition to the demands of recruitment, having a substantial part of the board stand down all at once presents problems of its own in terms of upheaval and sudden loss of institutional memory. Sometimes a senior trustee can be irreplaceable, particularly during times of crisis, as he or she can remember the last time such a thing happened and what the board did then. To get round this danger the board simply needs to retain for itself the power to make exceptions, then to use that power wisely and sparingly.

> *Sometimes a senior trustee can be irreplaceable, particularly during times of crisis...*

• At ActionRights it had been agreed that the gender imbalance needed to be corrected rapidly – there were too many males – and that the board should try to improve representation from non-British people, particularly appropriate people from countries in which ActionRights' programmes are based. Now ActionRights has quickly made substantial progress on both objectives.

• A minimum attendance rate is specified. If a trustee doesn't turn up for sufficient meetings he or she is asked to step down in favour of someone who will.

- The balance of skills sought by ActionRights is very clear. All trustees have to be generalists to some extent, but in addition it has identified the need for several with specific high level business experience, at least two senior financial managers, a lawyer, a media expert, a fundraising/marketing specialist, an IT expert and someone experienced in organisational effectiveness.

Of course ActionRights' board also has to have representation from a broad variety of leading figures in various fields of international development and poverty eradication. ActionRights now boasts a social policy and planning specialist, a professor of agricultural economy, a food security expert, an HIV/AIDS expert and a specialist in participatory development. All are world-renowned figures in their fields. There's just one specific vacancy, for a lawyer with human rights experience.

Why would anyone want to be a trustee?

Theresa explained that matching these strenuous and sometimes apparently conflicting requirements is a complex task that would challenge most headhunters (so far, ActionRights hasn't sought their services for this task, but it might yet). To match gender and ethnicity ambitions also and do it on an ongoing basis to satisfy frequent retirements is more than just a big job.

By now Warren was wondering why, with all these

conditions, anyone would want to be a trustee for ActionRights. Theresa's enthusiasm for her organisation seemed to grow as she spoke. 'Of course it's because of the fantastic work ActionRights does towards ending poverty', she exclaimed. 'But to make itself even more attractive to trustees, ActionRights has made real progress in reducing paperwork, has varied the times and style of board meetings, hosts occasional dinners for trustees, has an annual trustees' seminar and makes it possible for all trustees to see the agency's work for themselves by visiting projects in the field.'

Theresa went on to tell Warren that representation on the board from staff and beneficiaries (i.e the people ActionRights helps) is being considered but, for the time being at least, ActionRights won't contemplate paying trustees.

However, she added, 'That might need rethinking if the recruitment task becomes too difficult. But, although it is likely always to be a challenge, at the moment it seems probable that the charity will be able to find the quality, variety and number of new trustees it needs without having to call in specialist help, such as advertising in the press or using recruitment consultancies.

Some helpful hints

Theresa continued with helpful hints at such breakneck speed that Warren struggled to keep writing them down.

'Selecting people to serve on ActionRights' board

development committee is particularly important', she asserted. 'Obviously some HR/organisational development skills are appropriate, as are good contacts in a large number of fields. But the latter isn't essential as suitable contacts can be found elsewhere. The key qualities again are time, talent and commitment. You need people who want to find their own successors and who won't be satisfied unless they have a reasonable choice for every post.

'We've found it invaluable to give a dossier on the charity as an introductory pack to prospective candidates. This has to be excellent. Ours includes the annual report, our handbook for trustees, a couple of the Charity Commission's helpful free booklets and a video of the organisation's work. The whole package is not too bulky or too big a read, which helps.'

' ... candidates really do need to be sure before they commit themselves.'

Warren particularly noted Theresa's advice about not making candidates go through an over-rigorous selection process.

'The CEO and chair of the board development committee – it helps if the latter is also chair of the board – see each serious candidate. Two meetings are a must. All necessary detail is given in the first; questions answered and the candidate steered towards saying "yes" in the second. Overt persuasion isn't to be recommended. This is a voluntary position so candidates really do need to be sure before they commit themselves.

'Potential incoming trustees will welcome being asked to take on a finite job for a finite time. In my experience they will invariably appreciate a frank, realistic description of what's involved and the time they'll need to commit to do the job effectively. Nobody wants to be just a name on a letterhead these days. Such naked honesty may put a few folk off, but if so that's probably a good thing.'

Identifying the most likely

Warren asked how ActionRights finds suitable candidates. Theresa was characteristically forthright.

'We don't go after the most obvious or the most prominent, because everyone is after them', she explained. 'Finding trustees is time consuming and can be stressful, so you want to focus your approaches on people who you know match your criteria, and who are likely to say "yes".

'Really high-flyers may not make successful trustees. People at the top of their profession, or constantly in the media spotlight can have too many demands upon them to be effective trustees. The dilemma in identifying suitable new talent is that the most effective people are usually those with least time on their hands, whereas those who can readily spare the time may be idle for a reason. You have to be careful not to fill your board with mediocre people just because they are willing and available.

'The ideal candidate is someone rising in his or her career, looking for a social role, energetic and hard working with an interest in your work and time to give. Age should not be an issue – both retired and young people make excellent trustees. Some balance in ages is needed to ensure a good mix of energy, challenge and experience.'

Theresa explained that personality, or 'fit' is important. 'A balanced board will have a mix of boffins and extroverts, supporters and challengers, radicals and conservatives, or whatever suits your organisation. Board members should not all be alike and potential candidates should be assessed as to whether they will fit in with and complement the others.

'But', she warned, 'bear in mind that boards are frequently described as "an incompetent group of highly competent people", and getting a diverse group of eminent volunteers to work as a team is quite a task, particularly if you only have them together for a few hours each year.

'The board development committee is also a useful device for controlling recommendations of the "I know a good chap, just retired from the Army" variety. This still common approach inevitably leads to lookalike boards that are anything but representative. But at the same time, names gathered from existing trustees who can open doors can be really valuable, provided they are fed into an impartial selection process with clear, sound criteria and objectives. A good database is a must.'

Warren thought this sounded excellent good sense. Theresa's home station was coming up, so she began to gather her things. While handing Warren her business card and promising a follow-up meeting, Theresa gave her parting shot of good advice.

'The cornerstone of an effective recruitment policy... is the governance structure of the charity itself.'

'The cornerstone of an effective recruitment policy for new trustees is the governance structure of the charity itself. This needs to be clearly set out in a well-produced handbook detailing the charity's policy on all aspects of its governance from frequency, composition and conduct of meetings to powers and responsibilities of the board and its subcommittees, taking in all aspects of good governance on the way.

'I'll send you ours, so you can copy it', promised Theresa as she leapt from the train. Warren beamed his appreciation, once again.

The next challenge

With only minutes before his stop Warren thought about all he'd learned that day. 'This'll really shake up FuturePoint; perhaps we've dismissed too readily the trustees' bringing of the third T: treasure.'

Board members, Warren now realised, can and should help their causes in a vital and substantial way, among other things by playing their full part in the organisation's fundraising. There are many areas where they can have huge impact and provide inspirational leadership. Nowadays a generous gift rarely secures a seat on the board unless time, talent and commitment are also there in good measure.

As he gathered up his precious papers he thought of another frequently quoted 'three' of North American boards, which his new friend Theresa had told him about, the three Gs – give, get, or get off. 'This practice may not yet be widespread outside the USA,' he said to himself, 'and certainly hasn't been introduced at FuturePoint. So far. But perhaps that's the next challenge...'

Sources of guidance

England and Wales
The Charity Commission
There are several addresses depending on the size of your
organisation, the information you need, or your location. All
information on addresses and services can be found on:
www.charitycommission.gov.uk

The contact centre telephone number is:
+44 (0)845 300 0218

There is a minicom facility for hearing and speech-impaired
callers on: +44 (0)845 300 0219

Scotland
The Office of the Scottish Charity Regulator (OSCR)
Argyll House
Marketgait
Dundee
DD1 1QP
Tel: +44 (0)1382 220446; email: info@oscr.org.uk
www.oscr.org.uk

Northern Ireland
Department for Social Development
Castle Buildings
Stormont
Belfast
BT4 3PP
Tel: +44 (0)2890 569314; email: vcu@dsdni.gov.uk
www.dsdni.gov.uk/index/voluntary_and_community.htm

Other useful UK contacts
National Council for Voluntary Organisations
www.ncvo-vol.org.uk

Scottish Council for Voluntary Organisations
www.scvo.org.uk

Wales Council for Voluntary Action
www.wcva.org.uk

Northern Ireland Council for Voluntary Action
www.nicva.org.uk

National Association of Councils for Voluntary Service
www.nacvs.org.uk

Association of Chief Executives of Voluntary Organisations
www.acevo.org.uk

The Government's governance initiative
www.governancehub.org.uk

USA

BoardSource
1828 L Street NW
Suite 900
Washington DC 20036-5114
Tel: +1 (0)202 452 6262, or 877-89BOARD(877-892-6273)
www.boardsource.org

Canada

Imagine Canada (formerly Canadian Centre for
Philanthropy)
425 University Avenue
Suite 900
Toronto
Ontario M5G 1T6
Tel: +1 (0)416 597 2293, ext 229
www.imagine.ca

Association Resource Centre
151 Bloor Street West
Suite 800
Toronto M5S 1S4
Tel: +1 877 848 0240 (toll free in Canada and USA); or
+1 416 926 8780
www.associationconsultants.com

Australia

Nonprofit Governance Management Centre, Australia
PO Box 3872
Mansfield
NSW 2122
Tel: +61 2 9804 7960; email: boards@governance.com.au
www.governance.com.au

Acknowledgements

This book and its author owe a great deal to the help, support and professional input of many people, in particular my reviewers David Carrington, Jennie Thompson, Neil Sloggie, Harvey McKinnon, Rich Fox and Richard MacPherson. I also received invaluable input and advice from Pegg Nadler, Noerine Kaleeba, Alexandra Mitsotaki, Salil Shetty, Ramesh Singh and Karen Brown. Special thanks go to James Partridge, Claire Marley and their colleagues at the charity Changing Faces.

About the 'Tiny Essentials' series

The book you hold in your hands is part of a series of little books with a big mission. They focus on what really matters in one key area of voluntary sector management. Each book's purpose is to provide the essentials of its subject in an entertaining, easily digestible form, so people who otherwise wouldn't dream of reading a business book can effortlessly and enjoyably get access to what they really need to know.

Books in the 'Tiny Essentials' series are delightfully free of padding, waffle and over-blown theories. Extraneous material has been reduced to a minimum. Each book so lives up to its title that there's just no room for anything other than the essence of what really matters in the subject area, and how to order your priorities.

This 'Tiny' focuses on what every board member, CEO and senior nonprofit manager needs to know about managing a successful volunteer board. Other books in the 'Tiny' series include:

Tiny Essentials of Fundraising, by Neil Sloggie.

Tiny Essentials of Writing for Fundraising, by George Smith.

Tiny Essentials of Major Gift Fundraising, by Neil Sloggie.

Tiny Essentials of Raising Money from Trusts and Foundations, by Jo Habib (to be published in 2006).

Tiny Essentials of an Effective Fundraising Strategy, by Maggie Taylor (to be published in 2006).

Tiny Essentials of Monthly Committed Giving, by Harvey McKinnon (to be published in 2006).

All can be ordered at www.whitelionpress.com

A promise from
The White Lion Press

Enjoy the best books on fundraising and voluntary sector development.

Books by The White Lion Press will repay your investment many times over – and you'll enjoy reading them too. But if your purchase is damaged in any way, or if you feel any of our products do not live up to your expectations simply return them to us and we will issue you with a full refund, including any reasonable associated costs. We'll ask you to tell us why, so we can put right anything that might be wrong, but we won't quibble. Unfortunately we can only offer this if you bought the book directly from us, but even if you didn't, please let us know your problem and we'll do all we can to ensure your supplier matches our commitment to you. After all, you are our ultimate customer.

This guarantee applies to any books or videos you may purchase from us. We further promise to handle your orders with speed, efficiency and impressive politeness.

You can order further copies of this book, or any other titles, from our secure website, www.whitelionpress.com

Tiny Essentials of Fundraising

by Neil Sloggie
Softback, 57 pp. ISBN 0-9518971-5-2

All you really need to know about
fundraising, in one tiny book.

Join Kate, an inquisitive and ambitious
new recruit to the fundraising profession,
as she sets out to uncover what really
matters in her chosen career by visiting
and asking three seasoned practitioners.
Like Kate you'll see as much to avoid as
to emulate in the first two encounters but you'll be
reassured and inspired as, in her final meeting, Kate discovers
an organisation that has really thought through its fundraising
strategy and approach, and shares with her – and you – the
essential secrets of fundraising success.

'A simple and truthful reminder of what's at the heart of effective
fundraising. How I wish someone had given me this book when I
was starting out all those years ago!'
Jan Chisholm, managing director, Pareto Fundraising, Australia.

'I was given a copy of the 'Tiny' book in Australia and was so
enamoured of the clear message it conveys that I ordered a special
edition to give to more than 1,500 fundraisers and all 700 Blackbaud
employees. Their reactions have been universally positive. *Tiny
Essentials of Fundraising* is one of those books that make us truly
envious of the author for executing such a brilliant piece of
writing...'
Robert Sywolski, chief executive, Blackbaud Inc, USA.

'It's a smart idea, well-executed – how fabulous to have a bite-sized
book that sums up what makes for successful fundraising in such an
accessible way to both native and non-native English speakers.

'Great stuff. Thanks Neil for what must be the shortest, simplest
and yet very salient contribution to the world's literature on
fundraising.'
Julie Weston, UNHCR, Switzerland.

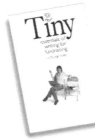

Tiny Essentials of Writing for Fundraising

by George Smith
Softback, 65 pp. ISBN 0-9518971-6-0

'I suggest your heart would soar if – once in a while – you received a letter written in decent English which said unexpected things in elegant ways, which moved you and stirred your emotions, which angered you or made you proud, a letter apparently written by one individual to another individual. For you never see these letters any more…'

If you believe that words matter then this opinionated little book is for you. For this 'Tiny' book will change forever the way you and your organisation communicate.

'*Tiny Essentials of Writing for Fundraising* is a refreshing – and delightfully short – guide to the author's insights about the writer's craft. If you're even thinking about writing fundraising letters you can't afford not to buy this remarkable little book.'
Mal Warwick, chairman, Mal Warwick & Associates Inc, USA.

'I am a huge fan of George's blunt but refined writing, his clear and individual voice, and his extraordinary ability to cut through the crap – keep this wonderful little book next to your pen and pc.'
Lyndall Stein, CEO, Concern, UK.

'Smith is a self-confessed curmudgeon but nobody describes better than he the power of words to advance your cause. The 11,149 words in this lovely book have been carefully selected and assembled to help you write well enough to convince anyone of anything.'
Ken Burnett, author, *Relationship Fundraising*; chairman, The Cascaid Group, UK.

Tiny Essentials of Major Gift Fundraising

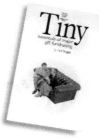

by Neil Sloggie
Softback, 61 pp. ISBN 0-9518971-7-9

The natural successor to his first book, *Tiny Essentials of Fundraising*, this time Neil Sloggie tells the story of Daniel, who had never thought of asking any donor individually for money, nor of asking for more than a three-figure sum. Join him in his search to uncover the Holy Grail of major gift fundraising and learn as he did how to secure donations bigger than a house – and lots of them.

This 'Tiny' contains in their purest, most distilled form the priceless secrets of a neglected area of vast fundraising potential.

'Help is close at hand in this small gem – wise counsel, the importance of colleagues and networking, heaps of practical advice. To borrow Neil's words, "keep this one near the top of your priority pile".'
Sue-Anne Wallace, chief executive officer, Fundraising Institute-Australia.

'... a really helpful guide, especially to someone just starting out or wishing to do a quick reappraisal of their operation.'
Nick Booth, campaign director, NSPCC 'Full Stop' campaign, UK.

'... very accessible and conversational... a must for all those considering or involved in this form of fundraising.'
Maggie Taylor, consultant and trainer, UK.

Relationship Fundraising: A Donor-based Approach to the Business of Raising Money (second edition)

by Ken Burnett
Published by Jossey-Bass Inc in association with The White Lion Press Limited. Hardback, 384 pp.
ISBN 0-7879-6089-6

Ken Burnett has completely revised and updated his classic book *Relationship Fundraising*. Filled with illustrative case examples, donor profiles, and more than 200 action points, this ground-breaking book shows fundraisers how to:

• Implement creative approaches to relationship-building fundraising.

• Avoid common fundraising errors and pitfalls.

• Apply the vital ingredients for fundraising success.

• Build good relationships with donors through marketing.

• Achieve a greater understanding of donors.

• Communicate effectively with donors – using direct mail, the press, television, the telephone, face-to-face contact, and more.

• Prepare for the challenges of twenty-first century fundraising.

'Not since Harold Seymour's classic, *Designs for Fund Raising*, has a book of this magnitude come along.

'Ken Burnett's updated and expanded work, *Relationship Fundraising*, just may be the book to which fundraising professionals turn for the next several decades.

'It is as brilliant as it is heartfelt, as simple as it is eloquent.'
Jerry Cianciolo, *The Compleat Professional's Library*, *Contributions Magazine*, USA.

'Ken Burnett's observations, insights and practical tips for building and sustaining relationships are superb. Highly readable, this book is a solid mix of sound theory and pragmatic application.'
Kay Sprinkel Grace, author, *Beyond Fund Raising*; co-author *High Impact Philanthropy*, USA.

'This is the book that sets the agenda for fundraising communications in the twenty-first century. Engaging, inspiring, and thought-provoking, *Relationship Fundraising* is based on the unique 25-year experience of one of the world's most respected fundraisers.'
Bernard Ross, director, The Management Centre, UK; co-author, *Breakthrough Thinking for Nonprofit Organizations*.

Friends for Life: Relationship Fundraising in Practice

by Ken Burnett
Hardback, 599 pp. ISBN 0-9518971-2-8

Amid the widespread acclaim that greeted the 1992 publication of Ken Burnett's *Relationship Fundraising* was one persistent qualified comment. Essentially the question was 'relationship fundraising sounds very attractive, but will it help us raise more money?'

In this accessible and entertaining sequel, Ken Burnett describes how relationship fundraising is working in a wide variety of organisations in the USA, Canada and the United Kingdom. Their stories provide the answer: a loud and resounding 'yes!'

But the ideas and experiences described in this book will do much more than just help fundraisers raise more money. They will show them how to develop and maintain strong, healthy, mutually beneficial relationships with their donors; relationships that will enable them to make friends for life.

The sequel to *Relationship Fundraising* first appeared in 1996, to international acclaim.

'I'm an enthusiastic fan of Ken Burnett's approach to building friends for life. His new book builds on the practical, common-sense approach to donor development he is famous for advocating.

'Great examples, an easy read – I highly recommend *Friends for Life: Relationship Fundraising in Practice*.'
Dr Judith E Nichols, CFRE, author and consultant, USA.

'Friends for Life is a witty, readable tour of donor-think from both

sides of the Atlantic and brings together a unique collection of experiences and anecdotes from many world-class fundraisers. *Relationship Fundraising* is already a classic throughout the world and this sequel is sure to have a similar impact.'

Jennie Thompson, consultant and co-founder of Craver, Mathews, Smith and Company, USA.

'The Botton Village case history is riveting. Its lessons have a relevance beyond fundraising. This is what direct marketing should always be, but so seldom is.'

Graeme McCorkell, author and consultant, UK.

Asking Properly: The Art of Creative Fundraising

by George Smith
Hardback, 220 pp.
ISBN 0-9518971-1-X

You will never read a book quite like this. George Smith tears open the conventional wisdom of fundraising creativity and so changes the rules for an entire trade. This book is irreverent, funny, savagely critical and genuinely inspiring, often on the same page.

Asking Properly is almost certainly the most authoritative book ever written about the creative aspects of fundraising. It is likely to remain a key text for years to come.

The author offers a profound analysis of donor motivation and is critical of the extent to which charities take their supporters for granted. But this book is no mere commentary on current practice – it offers a comprehensive checklist on how to optimise the creative presentation of the fundraising message. How to write, design, use direct mail, press advertising, broadcast media and the telephone, how to think in terms of fundraising products... the whole gallery of creativity and media is surveyed and assessed, with hundreds of examples of fundraising campaigns from around the world illustrating the need to 'ask properly'.

The book will prove invaluable to anyone involved in the fundraising process. It is provocative, entertaining and, above all, highly instructive. Read it, apply its lessons and it must enable you to raise more money.

'This book will become a classic. It's not just inspirational and a great read, there's a practical benefit on every page. When you apply George Smith's secrets you can hardly fail to improve your fundraising.'
Harvey McKinnon, president, Harvey McKinnon & Associates, Canada.

'It's typically George Smith: wise, uncompromising, devastatingly critical of poor fundraising, brilliantly illustrative of what is good, full of ideas, funny, marvellously written – and exceptionally good value. In short, *Asking Properly* is one of those very few books you will keep for life.'
Pierre-Bernard Le Bas, head of fundraising, UNHCR, Switzerland.

Friends for Life video series

A series of half hour videos from the Friends for Life sessions featuring Ken Burnett in Vancouver, Canada in July 1996. Filmed by Canada's Knowledge Network and produced jointly by Harvey McKinnon & Associates and The White Lion Press.

Video One

• The challenge of relationship fundraising.

• How to introduce world-class donor service.

• Getting ahead of your competition.

Video Two

• Botton Village: the classic case history of superb relationship fundraising.

• How you can profit from your donor's will.

• Four highly successful fundraising programmes.